chocolate

RYLAND
PETERS
& SMALL
LONDON NEW YORK

chocolate

DISCOVERING ★ EXPLORING ★ ENJOYING

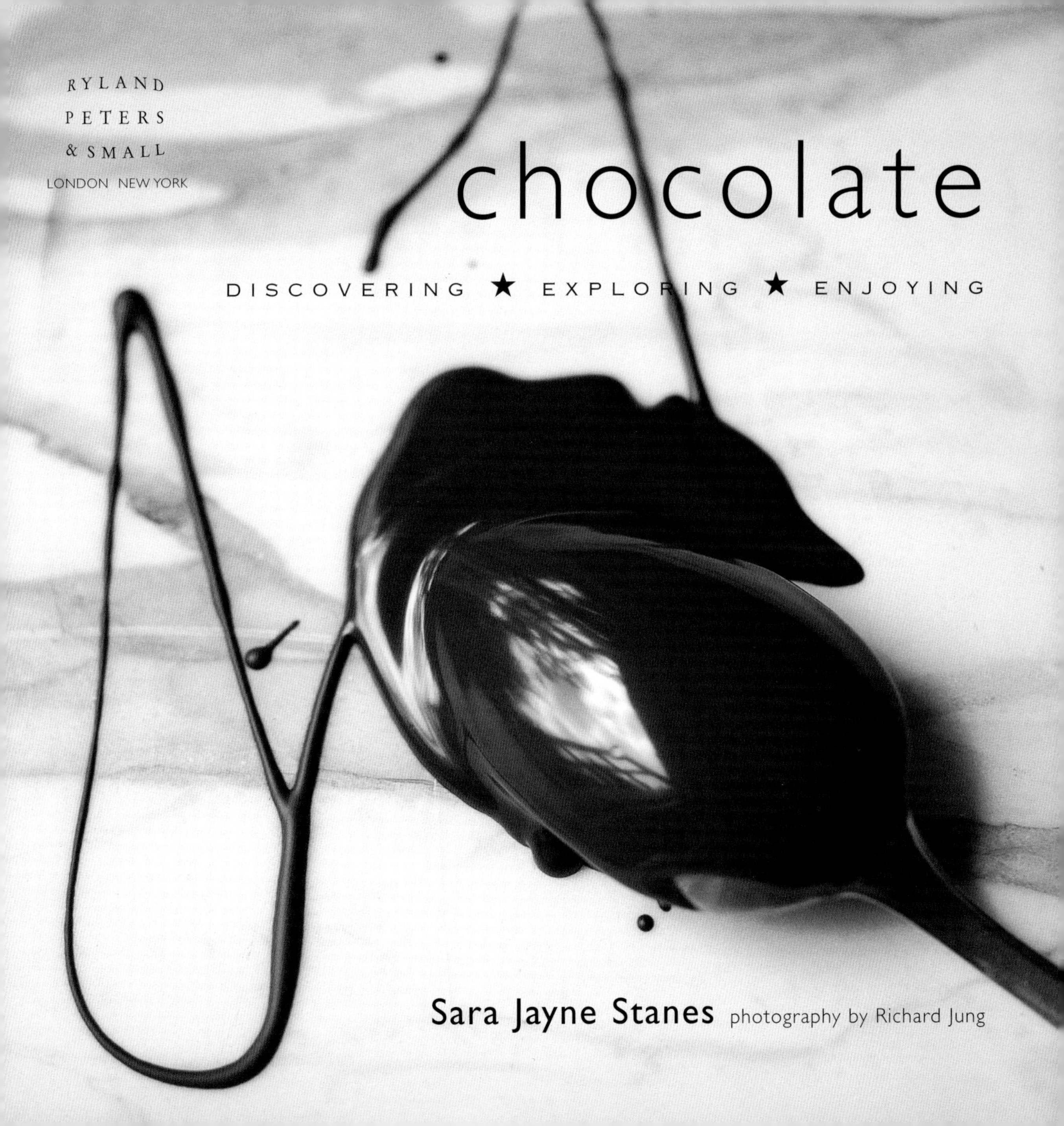

Sara Jayne Stanes photography by Richard Jung

SENIOR DESIGNER Steve Painter
EDITOR Sharon Cochrane
PICTURE RESEARCH Tracy Ogino
PRODUCTION Patricia Harrington
ART DIRECTOR Gabriella Le Grazie
PUBLISHING DIRECTOR Alison Starling

DIRECTORY Carole Bloom, CCP, author of *Truffles, Candies, & Confections: Techniques and Recipes for Candymaking* (Ten Speed Press, 2004), *All About Chocolate* (Macmillan, 1998), and six other chocolate and dessert cookbooks (www.carolebloom.com)

First published in the United States in 2005
by Ryland Peters & Small, Inc.
519 Broadway, 5th Floor
New York, NY 10012
www.rylandpeters.com

10 9 8 7 6 5 4 3 2 1

Library of Congress Cataloging-in-Publication Data

Jayne-Stanes, Sara.
  Chocolate : discovering, exploring, enjoying / Sara Jayne Stanes ; photography by Richard Jung.
     p. cm.
  Includes index.
  ISBN 1-84172-960-4
  1. Chocolate. 2. Chocolate--History. 3. Chocolate--Guidebooks. 4. Cookery (Chocolate) I. Title.
  TP640.J39 2005
  641.3'374--dc22
                         2005009616

Printed in China

contents

DISCOVERING

There is nothing else in the world like chocolate. Owing to the
nature of cocoa butter, chocolate is the only edible substance
that melts at around 93°F, just below body temperature. This
means that shortly after placing a piece of chocolate on your
tongue, it will begin to melt. Gradually your mouth will fill with
a softly erupting molten liquid, delivering a rainbow of flavors
that caress and tantalize the palate—a truly exclusive pleasure.

WHAT IS CHOCOLATE?

Chocolate, as we know it today, is a relatively modern manifestation. For thousands of years, cocoa beans were used only to make a drink. My first experience of this drink was in Mexico, where chocolate is still regularly consumed like this, according to customs and recipes handed down over generations going back 2,500 years. In the far south of Mexico, a family of Mayan women made chocolate for me in the traditional way. They ground the cocoa nibs using a *metate*—a concave stone made of volcanic rock—and a *metalpili*, a sort of pestle. They rolled the resulting soft mass until it yielded into a lump resembling a solid, unappealing, but divine-smelling clod of earth. They grated this rough substance, then added water to the shavings to make a drink.

This is how cocoa beans were used until the Industrial Revolution, around 1830, when technology intervened. Since then it has evolved to become the refined, creamy, edible substance that we now all know and adore.

THE ELEMENTS OF CHOCOLATE

The chocolate that we eat is made up of two main ingredients: beans from the *cacao* tree and sugar. The kernel (or nib) of the cocoa bean is roasted, then ground to produce cocoa mass or cocoa liquor (known as cocoa solids when set). This cocoa mass consists of cocoa butter—a virtually liquid fat—and non-fat cocoa solids, which are the rest of the dark brown "bits" of the nib. In a chocolate that contains 70 percent cocoa solids, the other 30 percent will be sugar.

The aim of a good chocolate manufacturer is to create a product with pure, heavenly viscosity and an irresistible "mouthfeel." To achieve this, the mixture of cocoa mass and sugar is processed and refined to reduce the size of the particles in the chocolate to less than 20 microns—less than the width of a hair—so they are practically imperceptible on the tongue, giving the smoothest of finishes.

CHOCOLATE CRAVINGS

Many of us admit to craving chocolate or to being a "chocoholic." Some people have explained its attraction in terms of the effect chocolate has on the brain's chemistry. That's certainly part of the story, owing to the chemicals that occur naturally in cocoa, such as caffeine, theobromine, and phenylethylalanine, which are the same as those emitted by the brain when stimulated by the thrills of a love affair, for example.

However, commercial chocolate usually contains such low amounts of cocoa solids that it is more likely to be the sugar to which most chocolate lovers are addicted, not the chocolate itself … and sugar is my *bête noire*. The inclusion of sugar in chocolate is acceptable in very judicial amounts, but when it is used as the principal ingredient—which is all too often the case—it completely disguises the true tastes of the chocolate. And tastes there are in abundance: the cocoa bean naturally contains almost 300 different flavors and 400 separate aromas. Did you ever dream our precious chocolate was so complex?

THE HISTORY OF THE COCOA BEAN

1500 to 400 B.C. Cocoa—or *cacao* as it is called by those who farm it—has been around for millions of years and is probably one of the oldest of nature's foods. Its native home is around Central and South America where it grew wild during the time of the Olmecs, the first of the recorded ancient civilizations of Mexico who lived in and around Veracruz from 1500–400 B.C. It is widely believed that the Olmecs were the first people to cultivate cocoa.

600 B.C. to A.D. 800 The Maya, another Mesoamerican people, whose land spread across the southern states of modern Mexico and Guatemala, have been credited with finding the most uses for cocoa. They used it principally for ceremonial rites and festivities, and also, importantly, as a restorative and cure-all. The Mayans were the first people to use cocoa as a gift. There would often be a reciprocal exchange of cocoa beans between bride and groom as a prenuptial acknowledgement to ensure that they lived a happy, healthy, and exemplary life in the eyes of their gods. The gods themselves were kept well and truly satisfied with cocoa beans which were often used in sacrificial rites.

A.D. 900 Another important civilization in the history of cocoa was the Toltec people, whose power climaxed about this time. They believed that the god Quetzalcoatl (*Ketzal-ko-atl*), depicted as a feathered serpent, came to earth on a moonbeam and brought the cocoa seed with him. He planted the seed, cocoa trees flourished, and he taught the people how to use the beans and how to benefit from their health-giving

qualities. However, the other gods were furious at Quetzalcoatl for sharing their heavenly manna with the "ordinary" people and subsequently, through trickery, they exiled him. As he fled, he vowed to return one day as a "fair-skinned, bearded man to save the earth."

1502 was the year that the first European was believed to have encountered cocoa. The Spanish-sponsored Italian explorer, Christopher Columbus, landed on the island of Guanaja off the coast of Honduras on his fourth and final voyage to discover India. As was customary in those parts, he was offered gifts by the natives. Apparently, one of those gifts was a basket of precious beans. The Spanish, of course, did not recognize cocoa beans and had no word for them. Columbus mistook them for old, shriveled almonds and so they went more or less unrecorded.

In 1518, Hernando Cortés—a Spanish explorer sent to conquer the Aztec empire—arrived in Mexico. He marched through appalling and hostile conditions from Veracruz to the Aztec capital, Tenochtitlan, to meet Montezuma—the penultimate in a long line of Aztec Emperors. A dynamic and fiercely proud man, Montezuma has become immortalized for the vast quantities of foaming *xoco atl* (chocolate) he drank before visiting his harem of wives, a practice which started the legend of the aphrodisiac qualities of chocolate.

When Montezuma met Cortés, his intuition told him that Cortés was the enemy. However, this was at odds with his religious beliefs, which partly convinced him that the white man with a beard, Cortés, was their god and

saviour Quetzalcoatl returning from the wilderness. Despite his reservations, Montezuma showered Cortés with gifts—including cocoa beans. Unfortunately, he should have listened to his first instincts. His people, appalled at this apparent betrayal, revolted and Montezuma was crucified. Cortés and his Spanish soldiers went on to destroy most of the Aztec nation.

It was during their time in Tenochtitlan that the Spanish became familiar with cocoa. It was called *xoco atl* by the locals, which, roughly translated, means bitter water. The Spanish originally thought it wasn't fit for pigs, but they had no choice but to get used to it because the local water made them sick and there was no wine in Mexico. Cocoa, however, was scarce. It didn't grow as far north as Tenochtitlan and had to be imported from the sacred cocoa plantations of Soconusco, in the far south of Mexico. As a result, it was used only by the titled and the rich, and on the occasion of religious ceremonies.

Furthermore, the Spanish discovered that the cocoa bean was used as a currency, making it even more valuable— 100 beans might buy a slave, while a rabbit might cost 30.

All of the Mesoamerican people knew that *xoco atl* was great for improving low energy levels and for stimulating brain power. There is no record of chocolate being eaten at this time, it was always consumed in liquid form. It was made as I have described on page 9, using a *metate* and a *metalpili* to crush and grind the beans to a paste. Sugar—unknown in this part of the world at the time—wasn't part of the recipe. However, an assortment of local herbs and spices was often added. When it was made into a drink with cold water, it was poured from a great height back and forth, from goblet to goblet, for several minutes in order to create a frothy surface.

During the late 1520s, Cortés took cocoa back to the Spanish court where its success was limited. Sugar had influenced the palates of the Europeans by this time and "sweet" had become the gastronomic key, so this bitter water was not immediately appealing. In addition, the tax imposed on the beans by the Spanish government was so extortionate that, like the ancient Mexicans, only the privileged could afford it. However, for reasons of court fashions, but more thanks to its perceived medicinal properties, chocolate did gradually become popular with Spanish royalty and their courtiers. Towards the end of the sixteenth century, chocolate workshops began to spring up in Spain.

In 1615, cocoa's most notable royal evangelist was Anne of Austria, daughter of Philip II of Spain. When she married Louis XIII, she took her precious cocoa beans to France with her and the French court fell in love with them.

However, it was the missionaries, sent out across the Atlantic to convert the natives of the New World, who brought back to Europe the knowledge of cocoa's many medicinal benefits. Reports of its "magical" and curative powers reached extraordinary proportions. Chocolate— a European corruption of *xoco atl*—was the elixir of life, a panacea for everything from headaches and stomach upsets to skin complaints and a cure for fevers and chills.

It was the nuns of Puebla in Mexico who were credited with the idea of adding sugar to cocoa in the mid-seventeenth century. Sugar was being grown in the West Indies at the time when the first cocoa was planted there and they thought by adding it, the drink was made far more palatable.

Around 1650, chocolate (along with tea and coffee) made its way to England, and the chocolate houses of London were born. These provided a focus for broadcasting the news of this great drink. It was still taxed so highly that, like in the New World and the rest of Europe, it was available only to those with money.

For the next 200 years, although its use in pastry and confectionery recipes started to creep into recipe books of the time, chocolate was mostly drunk for its physiological and mood-enhancing benefits. Consequently, it became one of the most important medicines in the apothecary's armory, which is the foundation for the great interest taken in it by the Quakers. Quakers were regularly to be found as apothecaries, partly because many of the other trades, universities (such as they were), and military activities were prohibited to them on moral and religious grounds. Subsequently, it was a group of Quakers who were responsible for turning chocolate into something more akin to the bars we know today.

CHOCOLATE AS WE KNOW IT

1729 Ever keen to improve the physical character of drinking chocolate, machinery was frequently being developed in an effort to make the drink smoother and more pleasing. During the early part of the eighteenth century, an English company called Walter Churchman, later bought by the great Joseph Fry, invented a water-powered engine to mill cocoa beans.

During the 1820s in Holland, Coenraad Van Houten patented the world's first cocoa press, which separated the cocoa butter from the cocoa powder. Shortly afterwards, he developed the alkalization of cocoa by adding potash—still known today as Dutching. He had seen this practice in Mexico when a Mexican Indian doctor mixed the wood ash of the fire with cocoa to make it more digestible.

In 1824, John Cadbury opened his first shop in Birmingham specializing in tea, coffee, and chocolate.

In 1847, based on these inventions, and in an effort to produce a smoother drink, the grandson of Joseph Fry discovered a way of mixing cocoa butter with cocoa paste to produce the world's first chocolate bar. It was really a by-product of the drink, but it took off and rather than using cocoa to produce a drink, it was soon found to be the most delicious, albeit extravagant food.

Quakers played a prominent role in the chocolate industry. The great family-run chocolate companies of the time were run by three Quakers: Joseph Storrs Fry (son of Joseph Fry), George Cadbury, and Joseph Rowntree. They created an immensely wealthy industry producing drinking chocolate as an alternative to the demon

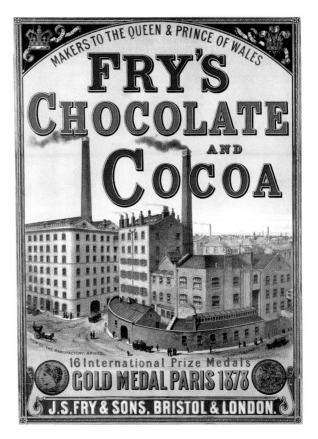

alcohol, gin in particular. They believed alcohol to be the cause of much of the misery and deprivation suffered by working people. They made a large contribution to the quality of chocolate and cocoa, while at the same time revolutionizing working conditions, not only in their factories, but also within the community. Bournville, the factory built near Birmingham by Cadbury, was intended to be a utopia for its workers. Likewise, Rowntree, Fry, and Terry (another Quaker) felt it essential to reward their workers with the best living and working conditions. This way not only did they fulfill their true philanthropic ethos, but it was also good for business.

In 1875, a Swiss man, Daniel Peter, discovered a way of mixing condensed milk, manufactured by his friend Henri Nestlé, with chocolate to create the first milk chocolate. In 1905, Cadbury's Dairy Milk was born.

In 1879, another Swiss man, Rudolphe Lindt, discovered conching—an essential process in refining chocolate (see page 21). He discovered this by accident when his assistant left a machine running all night.

In 1909, British Quaker chocolate companies, led by Cadbury, persuaded the chocolate makers of Europe to boycott cocoa from enslaved plantations in Portuguese West Africa. As a result of this historical episode, the British developed cocoa plantations along the Gold Coast (now Ghana), while the French planted cocoa seeds in the Ivory Coast. Today, over 80 percent of the world's cocoa beans are grown in Africa.

During the 1900s, all sorts of chocolate confectionery competed for the British palate. Products such as Fry's Turkish Delight, Cadbury's Fruit and Nut, Mars Bars, Flake, and Bounty Bars (like "Mounds" bars) all became household names. However, these products, which were becoming more adulterated with sugar, were a world away from the chocolate of their ancestors.

During this time, fine-chocolate lovers had to go to Europe to get their fixes. Belgian chocolate became king of quantity, while France dominated the quality market. However, the last two decades of the twentieth century witnessed an inspired revival of fine quality chocolate throughout Europe, from chocolate houses such as Cacao Barry—now Barry Callebaut—Valrhona, l'Opera, and Lindt, to the artisan companies such as Bonnat and Bernachon in France, Marcolini in Belgium, Green & Black's in the UK, and Amedei in Tuscany, whose ethics match its peerless chocolate. In the United States—not renowned for its fine chocolate—there are a number of small entrepreneurs endeavoring to raise the profile of good chocolate, such as Scharffen Berger and Dagoba.

WHERE AND HOW DOES COCOA GROW?

Cocoa pods grow on trees called *Theobroma cacao*, which means "food of the Gods." These trees are found in rain forests close to the Equator, between the latitudes of 20° North and 20° South. They grow to some 65 feet high in the wild, and between ten and 25 feet where they are cultivated. Today, the largest producers are the Ivory Coast, Brazil, Malaysia, Indonesia, and Ghana, while cocoa's original homes of Mexico, Venezuela, and Ecuador produce much less. However, South American cocoa is considered to be of the highest quality.

There are three main varieties of cocoa bean. The flavors of these beans—and therefore the chocolate that is made from them—are significantly influenced by the location, climate, and soil in which they are grown.

CRIOLLO

Meaning "native" or "of local origin," the Criollo bean is thought to be originally from Mexico. Nowadays, it is cultivated across Central and South America and in a few regions of Asia. True Criollo accounts for less than five percent of the world's cocoa production. It is considered to be the best cocoa with an unusually high aromatic profile that is substantially lacking in bitterness. It is used in the best quality chocolate but rarely alone because it is scarce and very expensive. It is finicky to grow and doesn't adapt well to different climates.

Pure Criollo is the subject of much debate among chocolate manufacturers and enthusiasts. Many say that, because of natural elements such as climate, weather, insects, and birds, it has been so cross-fertilized over the centuries that it has become an endangered species.

FORASTERO

This bean was originally from the Amazon and its name means "foreigner" or "stranger." It is a hardy variety that is now cultivated right across the global cocoa spectrum, from South America to Africa and from Malaysia to Indonesia. It accounts for 80 percent of the world's cocoa crop. The bean has a bitter flavor and is used in everyday chocolate.

TRINITARIO

The near total destruction of the Trinidadian Criollo plantations by a hurricane in 1727 led to the development of this bean—a hybrid of Criollo and Forastero. Forastero seeds for new plantings were brought to Trinidad from Venezuela and were cross-fertilized with the remaining native crop of Criollo. The resulting hybrid, Trinitario, had characteristics of both type of bean. It now accounts for 10 to 15 percent of the world's total cocoa bean crop. Trinitario is fine and rich in fats, has a good flavor profile, and makes exceptional chocolate.

HARVESTING THE PODS

Cocoa pods start their life as exquisite, minute, orchid-like flowers that grow on the lower branches and the trunk of the *Theobroma cacao*. The pods then emerge from these flowers.

Depending upon the variety, the pods may resemble ribbed rugby balls or lemons, and they appear in a rainbow of colors—from yellow and gold to brown, red, green, and mahogany. The pods, which contain between 25 and 40 seeds, weigh from seven ounces to 1¾ pounds and take five to six months to ripen. One tree produces only enough beans for 2¼ pounds of chocolate per harvest, of which there are two per year. The skill and experience of the cocoa farmer tell him when to harvest the pods, which is still done by hand with a machete.

When the pods are cut open, you will see the seeds, each one about the size of an olive. Together they form a giant "corn on the cob," covered in a milky white liquid. The taste of the freshly picked seeds resembles tropical fruit, like sweet lychees, pineapple, banana, and mango. After being exposed to the air for just a few hours, the seeds begin to oxidize. They become very bitter and inedible and start to develop their chocolate characteristics.

The seeds or beans are scooped out of the pods, piled in large heaps on the ground, and left to ferment. Depending upon the variety of the bean, fermentation will take between five and nine days. Fermentation is one of the most important stages of the cocoa bean's journey. This is when the germination of the seeds is arrested and the yeasts begin to convert the sugars—a similar process to that of wine. This leads to complex chemical changes, encouraging the chocolate flavors, aromas, and colors to develop.

Drying is also a very important stage that takes several days. Sun drying is preferable as doing this artificially can distort the flavors and aromas with smoke or other unwanted elements.

Once fermented and dried, the beans are packed into jute bags or loaded onto containers and shipped to the country of production.

ORGANIC CHOCOLATE

To be labeled organic, chocolate must be made from cocoa grown in plantations that have been free from chemicals and artificial fertilizers for at least five years. The manufacturing process itself must be certified organic, which means that no conventionally produced cocoa can be processed with the same machinery, unless it is thoroughly cleaned beforehand. Also, no unnatural additives can be used to make the organic chocolate.

One of the drawbacks of organic cocoa is that many of the varieties that have been cultivated over the years to produce the highest quality beans don't grow well without chemicals. Therefore the flavor and texture of the organic varieties can be variable. However, things are improving and there is now some very good organic chocolate available.

HOW CHOCOLATE IS MADE

Blending When the beans arrive at the point of chocolate production, the first thing that happens—in the case of most commercial chocolate—is that beans from different countries of origin are blended according to the manufacturer's recipe. The exception to this is "origin" or "single bean" chocolate, which, as the name suggests, uses only one type of bean. However, this high quality product represents only a small percentage of the total chocolate produced.

Cleaning and Roasting Next, the beans are cleaned to get rid of unwanted twigs and stones and then they are roasted. The roasting time and temperature are important to the end product. To save time, some manufacturers roast their beans at a higher temperature for a shorter time. The higher the temperature, the more bitter the chocolate and the more sugar is needed to mask the bitterness. Good quality chocolate relies on beans that are roasted at a lower temperature for a longer time, giving a flavor that is ultimately richer.

The beans are then winnowed to separate the nib from the shell. The shells are discarded and usually end up as garden fertilizer. The nibs—the vital element of chocolate—are then milled or ground. By refining the cocoa particles, the cocoa butter, which makes up 55 percent of the bean, is released and a liquid pulp is formed: cocoa mass. In its liquid state this is called cocoa liquor, as it cools and solidifies it is known as cocoa solids.

From here, the cocoa mass or liquor takes one of two journeys. It is either used to make chocolate or it is pressed to make cocoa cake and cocoa butter.

PRODUCING CHOCOLATE

Mixing and Kneading To make dark chocolate, sugar is added to the cocoa liquor and this is then kneaded into a dough. A good quality chocolate will consist of 70 percent cocoa solids and 30 percent sugar. To produce milk chocolate, different proportions of cocoa solids and sugar are used and milk powder is also added. White chocolate doesn't contain any cocoa solids, just cocoa butter (see page 21), milk solids, sugar, and vanilla.

Refining To make an unctuous, smooth chocolate, the size of the particles needs to be as small as possible. To achieve this, the dough is passed through a series of five revolving steel rollers. This reduces the size of the solid particles to 20 microns, or even smaller for top quality chocolate. By the time the mixture comes through the fifth roller, it is in powder or flake form and is barely perceptible to the touch.

Conching is an essential process that gives final smoothness to the chocolate. It is so-called because the paddles used in the first conching machines resembled shells, and "concha" is Spanish for shell. During conching, the chocolate mixture is constantly agitated and the friction of the paddles creates heat, which melts the mixture. More cocoa butter may be added at this stage to produce couverture chocolate, which is the very best chocolate you can find. The conching time should be long enough to homogenize the mixture and drive off the unwanted volatile aromas and bitterness, but not too long or some of the more complex chocolate flavors will be snuffed out. Not so long ago, it was a sign of a good chocolate when it was conched for four or five days. Modern technology has reduced the length of the process to eight or ten hours.

At this point, our chocolate is in liquid form and is either loaded onto thermostatically controlled tankers for distribution to industrial processors, such as bakers, confectioners, and cookie makers, or it is tempered (see page 22). Tempering ensures proper crystallization of the complex fats that make up cocoa butter and their homogeneous dispersal throughout the chocolate. Tempering is essential to produce the familiar "snap" and gloss of a good chocolate. Finally, the liquid chocolate is poured into molds to produce the ubiquitous blocks or bars.

PRODUCING COCOA POWDER AND BUTTER

The second route that the cocoa mass can take, other than to make chocolate, is to produce cocoa butter and cocoa cake. The cocoa mass is subjected to immense hydraulic pressure so that it separates to produce these two elements.

The cocoa cake is crushed into a fine powder and then alkalized (also known as Dutching, see page 14). Alkalization mellows the flavor and makes the powder more digestible by making it soluble.

The other element, cocoa butter, is an almost colorless vegetable fat that looks like pale olive oil. It is deodorized and refined for use in white chocolate and also added to some dark chocolate recipes.

THE CHOCOLATIER'S JOB

Many of us will buy chocolate in its simplest form—as a bar. But there are many delicious variations and ways with chocolate. If you walk into a specialty chocolate shop, you will see a whole host of tantalizing delights.

The chocolatier is the artist whose skills are those of a painter, sculptor, and architect with a degree in gastronomy, who will engineer the lightest, fluffiest, and tastiest of creations. He will whisk, fold, mold, and cajole the ingredients into truffles, pralines, cakes, and a larder full of other little pastries—a hedonist's imperative. A top pastry chef or chocolatier will train for many years before finally taking charge of a pastry department in a top hotel or restaurant.

TEMPERING CHOCOLATE

One of the trickiest tasks required of a chocolatier or pastry chef is the ability to temper chocolate. Tempering is required when melting chocolate for dipping or molding. The result must give a hard snap and an iridescent gloss. Tempering involves taking the couverture chocolate through a number of different melting and setting points to make sure that all the fat crystals are brought together "in chorus." If this isn't done properly, the chocolate will take a long time to set, it will not break cleanly, and it will be covered with a white bloom. The mouthfeel will also be different and therefore tastes will be obscured.

To temper chocolate, you need at least one pound of the best couverture and a digital thermometer. Grate one-fifth of the chocolate and chop the remainder into small pieces, about the size of half a walnut. Put the chopped chocolate in the top of a double boiler set over barely simmering water. Don't let the bottom of the top pan touch the water. Gently melt the chocolate, stirring occasionally so it heats evenly. When the chocolate is completely melted, give it one more stir and measure the temperature in the middle—it should be between 113°F and 118°F for dark chocolate, and between 111°F and 115°F for milk or white chocolate. Take care because if the temperature rises above 122°F, it may burn.

Remove the top pan from the heat and add the grated chocolate (leave the bottom pan barely simmering on the stove). Mix the chocolate thoroughly—this will help stabilize the cocoa fat crystals as well as help reduce the temperature to 80–82°F. You can place the bottom of the chocolate pan in cool water to help cool it down, but beware of introducing any water or steam into the chocolate. When the temperature reaches 80–82°F, put the chocolate pan back over the barely simmering water and, stirring gently all the time, bring the final temperature back to 88°F. Remove the top pan from the heat and use the chocolate immediately for dipping or molding. To check that you have tempered your chocolate correctly, dip the tip of a clean dry knife into the chocolate, then put the knife in the refrigerator for three to five minutes. The chocolate should be completely hard and shiny.

EXPLORING

One of my *bêtes noires* is that many chocolate-lovers do not
consider the difference between high-quality chocolate and
mass-produced confectionery. The word "chocolate" may be
used to refer to both of these products, but, in reality, they are
worlds apart. It's like comparing a cheap bottle of wine
with one of the very best vintages—they simply
aren't the same thing at all.

CHOCOLATE VARIETIES

The best quality chocolate will be defined by the variety of the cocoa beans used, where they were grown, and the fermentation and drying processes they have undergone. Once the beans have been chosen, the next most important part of the journey in the making of chocolate is the processing—the longer and slower, the better. Manufacturers of cheap, commercial chocolate, however, take a different view. Many cut corners by making their chocolate in the shortest possible time and with the cheapest ingredients, otherwise their profits would be severely challenged.

Extra-Bitter/Dark This contains at least 70 percent cocoa solids (the remaining 30 percent will be sugar). It's also likely that some lecithin and vanilla will be added. Check the label to see whether this is natural vanilla or an artificial flavoring. This will not only tell you more about the quality of the product, it will also affect the taste. Artificial vanilla will leave a chemical aftertaste.

Bittersweet This variety is similar to extra-bitter chocolate (see above), but it will have fewer cocoa solids, usually about 60 percent, and more sugar.

Semisweet The cocoa solid content of a good version of this chocolate is around 50 or 60 percent. Widely available commercial semisweet chocolate is legally required to contain a minimum of 35 percent cocoa solids and no more than 5 percent added vegetable fat. It will usually contain some other flavoring, such as synthetic vanilla, and lots of sugar. This will have an unexciting, claggy, undefined profile and eating quality.

Milk The cocoa solid content of milk chocolate varies considerably—a good quality milk chocolate will contain at least 32 percent. In my opinion, 40 percent or more is even better. The amount of milk solids will also differ between brands, but it is usually somewhere between 14 and 28 percent—this figure is often not indicated on the wrapper.

Widely available commercial milk chocolate is legally required to contain a minimum of 10 percent cocoa solids, about the same percentage of milk solids (you would probably never see more than 24 percent), and no more than five percent vegetable fat, which is often from a non-specified origin. Sugar will always be the most prominent ingredient.

White This consists of cocoa butter, milk solids, sugar, and vanilla flavoring—there are no cocoa solids. The better the quality of the chocolate, the more cocoa butter and less sugar it will contain. Of course, the vanilla will also be natural rather than a chemical flavoring.

Couverture With the addition of extra cocoa butter, any or all of the bars of eating chocolate mentioned on the opposite page could become couverture. Couverture is the finest chocolate that you can buy. It has undergone the most highly skilled, lengthy, and costly refining process and contains only cocoa mass, sugar, a minute amount of vanilla (if it is used at all), and lecithin. It is the addition of extra cocoa butter that makes the chocolate fluid when melted, which in turn makes it easy to use in the production of chocolate. This quality also makes it perfect for enrobing and helps to give the products a good shine. Couverture is also the very best chocolate to eat because it has a truly amazing melting quality in the mouth.

Unfortunately, I often see this top quality chocolate sold under the heading "cooking chocolate," when a more accurate description would read "chocolate for cooking." This can lead to confusion for a couple of reasons. "Cooking" chocolate in the UK and the United States is often a synthetic product that contains very little and sometimes no cocoa solids at all. I would avoid this product at all costs. This cheap "chocolate" is also known as "covering" chocolate because it is usually used to cover cakes and cookies. The name "couverture," when translated into English from the original French word, becomes "covering" which again leads to confusion between the best and the worst types of chocolate. Be aware of this and always check the label on the packet for the contents.

Gianduja This variety of chocolate is named after its Italian creator, Gian d'la Duja (*Jon-Dooja*), who first produced it in the latter half of the nineteenth century. It is a blend of either milk chocolate or, more unusually, dark chocolate and ground hazelnuts or sometimes almonds. As a result of the Napoleonic wars, cocoa was rationed in Italy at this time, so the addition of hazelnuts helped to make the scarce cocoa go further.

A WORD ABOUT QUALITY

How do you recognize a good chocolate? As with most good food, and as a basic principle, the more senses a chocolate appeals to, the better (see page 36).

COMMERCIAL CHOCOLATE

I believe we have been "tastewashed" by commercial chocolate, growing up on products where the true flavors of the beans have been gagged by the addition of lots of sugar. Like salt, sugar used in excess merely kills the taste and leaves an unpleasant aftertaste. Sugar also tends to be addictive.

THE BEST CHOCOLATE

The transition from commercial chocolate to the sophisticated high-cocoa-solid chocolate can be a shock to the system. My first experience made my eyes water. If you haven't discovered "pure" chocolate, take it slowly. It's an acquired taste. Now, I could no more eat a piece of the sugary chocolate confectionery of my childhood than eat the paper in which it is wrapped. Having said that, it is a matter of personal taste and there is, no doubt, room for both in a person's list of favorite foods.

We tend to define quality chocolate by its cocoa solid content. This works as a general rule, but it's not always the case. The quality will also depend on other factors, such as proper fermentation and drying, which are essential to the flavors and maturity of the beans as well as to the subsequent quantity of sugar needed. The best way to establish the quality of chocolate is by reputation and elimination by simple trial and error. Read the label to check that the ingredients are as natural as possible.

Chocolate is at its best when fresh and will not improve upon keeping, so always buy the freshest you can. If it smells stale, it will taste stale.

WHERE TO BUY IT

There are a number of places where you can buy
chocolate, but before you decide which one to visit,
you need to ask yourself precisely what it is you
are looking for. Is it a bar of dark, milk, or white
chocolate? Or a bar of sweet, mass-produced
confectionery? Or do you want the real thing? By
which I mean an artisan-created chocolate, praline,
or truffle, made with fresh ingredients and the best
quality chocolate. You will only find this specialty
product in a specialty shop. Because of the time
needed to make such an artisan product and the
necessary skills and experience involved, good
hand-crafted chocolate will be as expensive as its
equivalent in wine or cheese. So be prepared to
pay for quality and you will get what you pay for.

SUPERMARKETS

The range and quality of chocolate available in supermarkets
is improving, but you have to know what you are looking for
and how to navigate your way around the shelves. To provide
space in a cool cabinet for a true artisan-made box of
chocolates would be prohibitively expensive. As a result,
you are likely to find ranges from only the biggest industrial
chocolate producers. Having said this, some selected stores
now stock a few exceptional chocolate makers, such as
Valrhona and Green & Black's. If you are looking for
chocolate to use in cooking, the supermarket will be the
best place for quality chocolate at a good price.

Never buy "covering" chocolate (see page 27). It's a
"mechanical" product that usually contains no cocoa solids,
just synthetic chocolate flavoring and industrial ingredients.

FOOD HALLS IN DEPARTMENT STORES

Some department stores have food halls that are well worth a visit. They are excellent sources of a whole range of chocolates to suit a variety of palates and purses.

SPECIALTY CHOCOLATE SHOPS

This is where I am in heaven. Here you will find a whole range of exquisite artisan-crafted chocolates. The sales assistant should be *au fait* with the product and able to answer any questions. They should be able to communicate the passion and personality of the chocolate maker, too. Most good chocolate shops will have something that you can taste to give you a flavor of what's available.

Here you will find "origin" chocolate couverture bars made with a single variety of cocoa bean containing 60 to 75 percent cocoa solids, sometimes more. These bars are often mixed with such lavish and interesting ingredients as Szechuan pepper, chili, sea salt, cardamom, lavender, basil, and geranium.

There will always be truffles, made from the finest ganaches, using the best quality dark or milk couvertures. These may be flavored with anything from raspberries, peppers, and cardamom to eaux de vie and Scotch malt whisky.

You might find chocolate-covered prunes, marzipans, nuts, nougat, coffee beans, and crystallized orange and lemon peels. There will be pralines with nuts and caramels as well as rose and violet creams (once more seen on the most fashionable dinner tables). For making drinks, there will be cocoa with a high cocoa solid content, as well as "real" drinking chocolate.

MAIL ORDER AND WEBSITES

There are a growing number of mail order sources and websites that sell fine chocolate, putting quality products within everyone's reach. I have listed some of my favorite shops and other sources on page 62, but this list is by no means exhaustive. The best sources will be found by word of mouth and reputation.

ENJOYING CHOCOLATE AT ITS BEST

Always store chocolate in a cool, dry place. Only refrigerate it if it is wrapped tightly or stored in an airtight container—chocolate absorbs strong smells and hates damp atmospheres prevalent in fridges.

KEEPING CHOCOLATE

Dark chocolate can last up to twelve months, while milk and white chocolate will keep for up to nine. Always check the expiration date on the package. Dark chocolate lasts longer because the cocoa liquor used to make it contains natural antioxidants that act as a preservative.

PERSONAL TASTE

For reasons of personal preference and tradition, it has become customary to eat chocolate after a meal, which rather defeats the object. Purists claim that to taste the full profile and complexity of chocolate, you should never eat it after other foods. However, I love chocolate at all times of the day. The first piece in the morning, like the first cup of tea, is always special.

Like cheese, it is considered *de rigeur* to eat chocolate at room temperature, or it will fall short. For a dark chocolate bar, I totally agree. If it's too cold, it will not render its unique melt, and the taste and experience will suffer. However, I can think of nothing better than to take a bite of a cool chocolate truffle from the refrigerator and to let it melt slowly on the tongue, releasing its profusion of flavors—and, of course, it lasts longer.

My favorite chocolates vary and my choice will depend upon my mood, the time of day, and what I have eaten. I prefer eating dark chocolate in the afternoon, and truffles at the end of a fine dinner. I rarely approve of a chocolate with more than 70 percent cocoa solids, as I believe you need a minimum amount of sugar to balance the bitterness.

TASTING

There are good reasons to draw an analogy between wine and chocolate when tasting. Just as the variety and quality of the grapes, the soil, climate, fermentation, and the experience and knowledge of the wine maker are crucial to the wine, it is precisely so with chocolate. The variety of the bean, where it is grown, the soil, climate, fermentation, and recipe of the chocolate maker will all affect the taste.

FLAVORS AND AROMAS

There are many natural chemical compounds present in both the grape and the cocoa bean, and when you are tasting chocolate, especially dark, it is as well to remember that the cocoa bean boasts more than 400 aroma compounds and over 300 different flavors. As with wine, tasting chocolate is a very personal experience and there is no right or wrong. We all taste foods differently.

Since cocoa is a fruit, this will be the principal taste. In the powerful but perversely subtle dark chocolate, mingling with the red fruit you will find suggestions of leafy soil, spice, herbs, and flowers, all enveloped in that wonderful unique cocoa butter that is responsible for its extraordinary mouthfeel. As a guide you might detect any of these flavors: melon, citrus, orange flower, cherry, berries, plums, raisin, honey, peach, vanilla, butterscotch, toast, wild herbs, mint, bell peppers, freshly mown grass, hay, green olive, clove, licorice, cedar, almonds, hazelnuts, eucalyptus, exotic flowers, tobacco, jute, tea, coffee, and wine. Don't expect to detect more than three or four in any one chocolate. What you don't want to discover are unwanted flavors, such as smoke, fat, potassium, alcohol, acid, medicinal, cardboard, astringent, or stale.

I find it more difficult to detect as many flavors in milk and white chocolate as in dark because of the low cocoa content, the milk, and the overpowering presence of sugar, which kills tastes and aromas. Having said this, a number of manufacturers have improved their milk chocolate by using a higher proportion of cocoa solids, therefore less sugar, and these are worth hunting out.

THE FIVE SENSES

A good chocolate should appeal to all of the senses. The process of tasting chocolate is much the same as that of wine in that you need to consider such things as the color, aroma, and texture. When tasting, drink only water to keep the palate clean.

Sight Chocolate should look flawless, evenly colored, and a deep shade of mahogany or red. Black is not necessarily an indicator of a quality chocolate. Cocoa beans are rarely jet black; if they are, it tends to indicate they have been over-roasted. There should be no cracks, air pockets, streaks, or sugar bloom, which is caused when chocolate is subjected to various temperature changes.

Smell As you unwrap a chocolate, you should smell a complex fragrance. It should be sweetly fragrant but not overpowering. You might detect all sorts of gems from nature's larder (see page 35). It's bad to have no smell at all—if you can't smell, you can't taste. Burnt, musty, chemical, or medicinal aromas aren't good.

Touch It should feel silky, not sticky. It should just begin to yield to the warmth of your fingers. Remember, it's the only edible substance that melts at body heat.

Sound Break a piece. It should snap cleanly and shouldn't splinter or crumble. Take a look inside, it should be solid all the way through with no blemishes.

Taste Most of our taste buds are on the front of the tongue, which is where you should start tasting the chocolate. If it doesn't start to melt right away, this is probably a sign of poor quality (or it could just be that it is too cold—taste it at room temperature). Here comes the chocolate's biggest test; now should begin the taste explosion. It should be smooth and buttery, gently melting into a creamy liquid, filling the mouth with its complexity of flavors. It must not be grainy or "gluey." The sign of a really good chocolate is a long, clean, well-defined aftertaste that lasts and lasts for many minutes, like a good wine.

WHAT TO DRINK WITH CHOCOLATE

What happens in the mouth when you combine chocolate and alcohol can be truly astonishing, while sometimes it can be a perplexing misery. And it is not always the same for everyone. It can be difficult to find a partnership that works because combinations of wine and chocolate are infinite. It depends so much on trial and error because of all the natural flavor elements that make up chocolate's unique complexity. However, when choosing something to accompany your chocolate, there are a number of sensual elements to consider.

Dark Chocolate A simple partnership of a dark chocolate and a young Bordeaux wine can work well. This is because the chocolate and the wine both share a similar balance of the principal flavors of red berry fruits, as well as tannins and acidity. However, such a combination doesn't always work. A more predictable marriage is with a rich wine, such as a fine Banyuls or Maury from Roussillon in southwest France. Rich wines work so well with dark chocolate that they are often used by chocolate makers in their tastings.

Chocolate Desserts and Confectionery With so many additional flavors in a dessert or a confection, it can be difficult to find something to drink with it that doesn't put your palate under siege. A good choice is a port or Madeira, especially a vintage Sercial or Verdelho.

Truffles made with a diversity of flavors can pose problems. Here, you might want to try to match the flavors of the chocolate with the accompanying drink. For example, if you have a chocolate with a citrus flavor, the perfect partner may be an orange-flavored liqueur, such as Grand Marnier or Cointreau. Spirits such as gin and vodka are too harsh, but a fine malt whisky or cognac can definitely work.

Milk Chocolate The aromas of caramel, honey, and toasted hazelnuts in a milk chocolate can go particularly well with a sweet fortified wine that is low in tannins.

White Chocolate Finding a partner for white chocolate can be tricky. Its sweetness, coupled with its overpowering vanilla, fights with wine. My suggestion would be a sweet sparkling wine, such as an Asti Spumante, or an Essencia Orange Muscat from California.

THE BENEFITS OF CHOCOLATE

The good news is that chocolate is good for us—as long as it contains at least 60 percent cocoa solids (ideally more than 70 percent), has no added dairy products, and isn't overpowered with sugar. Raw cocoa beans or nibs are even better for us. Sadly, milk and white chocolate fans will have to look away—neither have the same benefits. Chocolate cakes and confectionery can't be described as healthy either.

THE GOOD NEWS

The Olmecs, Mayans, Toltecs, and Aztecs were keen to keep their gods supplied with chocolate, in the form of cocoa beans, to keep them happy and healthy. They also used *cacao* to treat fatigue, alleviate breathlessness and fever, to treat a faint heart, help an ailing liver or spleen, and to alleviate headaches and depression. We have also seen that Montezuma relied on his 50 cups of foaming *xoco atl* a day to keep up his stamina before visiting his harem. These much proclaimed medicinal uses of *cacao*, both as a principal remedy or as a way of conveying other medications, were part of the ancient customs of the Mesoamerican people going back thousands of years.

Since cocoa, in the form of a drink, was introduced to Europe and later to North America, its medicinal uses have been far-reaching. It has improved poor appetite, digestion, anemia, nervous disorders, mental fatigue, consumption (tuberculosis), fever, gout, and kidney stones. Cocoa beans and cocoa butter, as well as the bark, leaves, and flowers of the cocoa tree have all been used to treat burns, cuts, and skin abrasions.

The chocolate world's esteemed body, the International Cocoa Association, commissioned the International Research and Education Foundation to carry out independent research on the nutritional and health aspects of cocoa and chocolate. The study indicated that the overall picture is one of nutritional benefits.

Blood Pressure and Heart Disease Chemicals called flavanols, present in cocoa drinks and to a lesser extent in chocolate, can boost the production of nitric oxide. This chemical plays an important part in the maintenance of healthy blood pressure and, in turn, cardiovascular health. Research at Harvard Medical School has shown that the benefits of cocoa on blood pressure can be as great as those of aspirin.

Deep Vein Thrombosis The chances of developing this condition can also be offset by flavanols according to research at the University of California Davis. A two-ounce bar of chocolate contains the same concentration of these chemicals as two glasses of red wine, four cups of tea, six apples, or seven onions.

Cholesterol Stearic acid, chocolate's predominant saturated fat, is a unique fatty acid in that it has a neutral effect on blood cholesterol levels, and may even be able to lower them.

Antioxidants Dark chocolate, like wine, contains numerous antioxidants, which is why it keeps so well. They are also good for us.

Cough Recent gossip from the academic world suggests that the theobromine in chocolate can be a marvelous remedy for a cough.

ENJOYING

While chocolate is wonderful on its own, combining it
with other ingredients creates so many more inspiring ways
of enjoying the chocolate experience. My most valuable
tip when you are baking with chocolate is to remember
that the results of your labors will be directly proportionate
to the quality of the chocolate you choose. Always
use the best you can find.

Brownies are an eternal favorite with all ages. They are extremely versatile and can be eaten at any time of the day— they can even be served as the perfect ending to a dinner party, accompanied by vanilla ice cream or cream.

chocolate brownies

4 oz. dark chocolate (70 percent cocoa solids)

1 stick unsalted butter

2 large eggs

1¼ cups soft dark brown sugar

1 vanilla bean

⅔ cup all-purpose flour

1 teaspoon baking powder

¾ cup pecans, walnuts, or toasted hazelnuts, chopped

a cake pan, 8 inches square and 2 inches deep, buttered, and completely lined with parchment paper

MAKES 16

Break the chocolate into pieces and put them in a saucepan. Add the butter and heat gently over very low heat, stirring occasionally, until melted and smooth. Let cool while preparing the rest of the mixture.

Put the eggs and sugar in a large bowl. Cut the vanilla bean in half lengthwise and scrape the seeds into the bowl. Beat with a hand-held electric mixer until thick and creamy.

Sift the flour and baking powder into the egg mixture. Add the nuts, then fold in using a large metal spoon. Carefully fold in the melted chocolate mixture. Do not overmix or the brownies will be dry. Pour the mixture into the prepared cake pan. Bake on the middle shelf of a preheated oven at 350°F for 40 minutes or until a skewer inserted midway between the center and the sides of the pan comes out clean. The center should be just firm. Do not overcook or the brownies will be dry.

Remove from the oven and let cool completely in the pan. Lift the paper to remove the brownies, then cut them into 16 squares. Store in an airtight container for up to 1 week.

This is the richest chocolate recipe I know, but one of the most delicious. You will need only a sliver for full effect—definitely a case of less is more.

baked chocolate cake

21 oz. dark chocolate
(70 percent cocoa solids)

3½ sticks butter

4 extra-large eggs

⅔ cup sugar

sour cream or ice cream,
to serve (optional)

*a removable-bottomed cake pan,
10 inches diameter, lined with
parchment paper and buttered*

SERVES 6

Break the chocolate into pieces and put them in a saucepan. Add the butter and melt gently over very low heat, stirring occasionally, until melted and smooth. Let cool.

Put the eggs and sugar in a large bowl and beat with a hand-held electric mixer until three times the original volume. Add one-quarter of the melted chocolate mixture to the bowl and, using a plastic spatula, mix gently until thoroughly incorporated. Add the remaining melted chocolate and fold in gently until well mixed.

Pour the batter into the prepared pan and bake in a preheated oven at 325°F for 8 minutes. The cake will still be slightly soft to the touch, not firm. Don't be tempted to cook it for any longer than this. Remove from the oven and let cool in the pan. Serve cold with a dollop of sour cream or a scoop of your favorite ice cream, if you like.

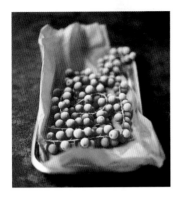

Thanks to Mark Hix for generously sharing this wonderful idea. It is the perfect combination of unsweetened frozen fruit and sweet, creamy white chocolate sauce. Use your favorite berries, or a mixture, and choose good quality white chocolate or the sauce will be too sweet.

frozen seasonal berries with white chocolate sauce

2 lb. fresh mixed berries

1 lb. good quality white chocolate, finely chopped

2½ cups whipping cream

a baking tray

SERVES 8

Lay out the berries on a baking tray and open-freeze them for 2 to 3 hours. Alternatively, you can use the ready-frozen mixed berries available from most supermarkets.

Put the chocolate in a large heatproof bowl.

Put the cream in a saucepan and heat it very gently until it boils. Remove the pan from the heat and, when the cream has subsided, pour a small amount over the chocolate. Stir well until thoroughly mixed, then add the remaining cream, a little at a time, mixing thoroughly after each addition.

Pour the mixture back into the pan and heat very gently until it just reaches simmering point—under no circumstances must it boil. Remove the pan from the heat.

Scatter the frozen berries on 8 individual plates and pour the hot white chocolate sauce over them. Alternatively, serve the sauce separately for your guests to pour themselves. Serve immediately.

For a silky smooth texture, make sure the chocolate, gelatin, and egg yolk mixture is still warm when folded together, before adding the cream.

chocolate marquise

9 oz. dark couverture chocolate (70 percent cocoa solids), broken into pieces

3 sheets of leaf gelatin

3 large egg yolks

2 tablespoons sugar

2 tablespoons brandy (optional)

1¾ cups whipping cream

unsweetened cocoa powder, for dusting

light cream, to serve

a nonstick, 1 lb. loaf pan, greased and lined with 2 long strips of parchment paper so the ends hang over the 4 edges of the pan

SERVES 6

Put the chocolate pieces in the top of a double boiler set over simmering, but not boiling, water (do not let the bottom of the pan touch the water). Melt the chocolate gently, stirring occasionally, until smooth. Remove the top pan from the heat and let the chocolate cool slightly.

Put the gelatin sheets in a small saucepan and cover with cold water. Let soak for 3 minutes until soft, then drain off the water. Heat the gelatin over very low heat, swirling the pan, until the gelatin dissolves. Set aside.

Put the egg yolks in a large heatproof bowl and beat with a hand-held electric mixer until pale and creamy.

Put the sugar and ¼ cup water in a small saucepan and heat gently until the sugar has dissolved. Increase the heat and cook for 3 minutes or until the temperature of the water has reached 240°F—check with a sugar thermometer. Gently pour the sugar syrup onto the egg yolks, beating with a hand-held electric mixer as you pour, until the mixture becomes thick and creamy. Beat in the brandy, if using. Add half the warm chocolate and stir well with a large metal spoon until well mixed. Gently stir in the remaining chocolate, followed by the warm gelatin.

Put the cream in a bowl and whisk until it starts to thicken. Using a large metal spoon, gently fold the cream into the chocolate mixture. Pour the mixture into the prepared loaf pan, tapping the bottom gently on the counter so the mixture reaches the corners. Level the top with a knife. Cover and chill in the refrigerator overnight until set.

When ready to serve, gently lift the marquise out of the pan by pulling up on the parchment paper and transfer to a serving plate. Dust with cocoa powder, then cut into thick slices. Serve with a drizzle of cream.

For a dinner party, put the fresh raspberry purée in the bottom of attractive wine glasses and pipe the mousse over the top.

white chocolate mousse

4½ oz. white couverture chocolate, broken into pieces (about ¾ cup), plus ½ oz., finely grated

1½ sheets of leaf gelatin

¼ cup sugar

2 large egg whites

1 teaspoon raspberry framboise (eau de vie), optional

1¼ cups whipping cream, whisked until it starts to thicken

RASPBERRY PURÉE

14 oz. fresh raspberries

confectioners' sugar, to taste

6–8 wine glasses or glass dishes

a nonstick baking tray

SERVES 6–8

To make the raspberry purée, put the fruit in a blender, with confectioners' sugar to taste, and whizz until smooth. If you prefer a smooth result, push the raspberry purée through a fine-mesh nylon strainer to remove the seeds. Divide the purée among the glass dishes.

Put the chocolate pieces in the top of a double boiler set over simmering, but not boiling, water (do not let the bottom of the pan touch the water). Melt the chocolate gently, stirring occasionally, until smooth. Remove the top pan from the heat and let the chocolate cool.

Put the gelatin in a small saucepan and cover with cold water. Let soak for 3 minutes until soft, then drain off the water.

Meanwhile, spread the sugar on a nonstick baking tray and warm it in a preheated oven at 325°F for 5 minutes. Put the egg whites in a large bowl, add half the warmed sugar, and beat with a hand-held electric mixer until stiff peaks form. Beat in the remaining sugar until the mixture is shiny and smooth. Whisk in the framboise, if using.

Heat the softened gelatin over very low heat, swirling the pan, until it dissolves. Add it to the beaten egg whites and stir gently with a large metal spoon to mix. Gently fold in the cooled chocolate, then fold in the whisked cream until the mixture is smooth. Finally, stir in the grated chocolate.

Spoon the mousse on top of the puréed fruit. Alternatively, for a special occasion, pipe the mixture from a large pastry bag fitted with a wide, plain nozzle. Chill in the refrigerator for at least 30 minutes before serving.

Variation Replace the raspberry purée with a prune version, if you prefer. Put 2 cups soft pitted prunes in a saucepan with 1 cup weak Earl Grey tea and simmer for about 10 minutes until soft and most of the liquid has been absorbed. Transfer to a blender and whizz until smooth. Continue as above.

The point of these wonderful desserts is that the center is still blissfully liquid when you serve them, so don't be tempted to cook them for any longer than the stated time. They are delicious served on their own or with ice cream.

little hot chocolate mousses

5 large eggs, plus 5 large egg yolks

½ cup sugar

8 oz. dark chocolate (at least 70 percent cocoa solids), broken into tiny pieces

1¾ sticks unsalted butter

½ cup all-purpose flour

½ cup unsweetened cocoa powder, plus extra for dusting

ice cream, to serve (optional)

8 ramekins, buttered, or nonstick dariole molds

SERVES 8

Put the eggs, egg yolks, and sugar in a large bowl and beat with an electric hand-held mixer until the mixture is pale yellow, 10 to 15 minutes.

Put the chocolate and butter in the top of a double boiler set over simmering, but not boiling, water (do not let the bottom of the pan touch the water). Melt gently, stirring frequently, until smooth. Remove the top pan from the heat. Add a small amount of the egg and sugar mixture to the melted chocolate and stir until well mixed. Add the rest of the egg mixture and mix well. Sift the flour and cocoa powder into the bowl and gently fold it in with a large metal spoon until just mixed.

Stand the prepared ramekins or molds in a roasting pan to stabilize them and spoon the mixture into them (the mixture should come to just below the rim of the molds).

Bake on the middle shelf of a preheated oven at 350°F for 10 to 12 minutes until risen and just firm to the touch. Don't cook them any longer than this or they will set inside.

Run a round-bladed knife around the inside of each mold to loosen the desserts, then carefully turn them out onto individual plates. Dust with cocoa powder and serve immediately, either on their own or with your favorite ice cream.

This is my favorite recipe for chocolate. I adore ice cream in any form. For me, the perfect summer's afternoon (well, to be truthful, any afternoon) isn't complete without a double cone of vanilla and chocolate ice cream.

chocolate ice cream

1 cup light cream or whole milk

10 oz. dark chocolate (70 percent cocoa solids), finely chopped (about 2 cups)

⅓ cup sugar

6 large egg yolks

3 cups whipping cream

an ice cream maker (optional)

SERVES 10

Put the cream or milk in a saucepan and bring to a boil. Remove the pan from the heat and stir in the chocolate until melted and smooth.

Put the sugar and egg yolks in a bowl and beat with a hand-held electric mixer until thick and creamy, about 10 minutes.

Put the whipping cream in a saucepan and bring to a boil. Remove the pan from the heat and pour the hot cream onto the sugar and egg mixture. Stir well to mix. Rinse the pan, then pour the mixture back into it. Heat over very low heat, stirring all the time with a wooden spoon, until the mixture coats the back of the spoon. Do not let the mixture boil or it will curdle.

Pour the mixture through a fine-mesh strainer into a large bowl. Add the melted chocolate mixture and mix until smooth. Let cool completely, then chill in the refrigerator.

Churn the chilled custard mixture in an ice cream maker, following the manufacturer's instructions, until frozen. Transfer to a freezerproof container and freeze until ready to serve. Alternatively, to freeze without a machine, pour the mixture into a shallow plastic container and freeze it. When almost solid, beat it with a hand-held electric mixer until smooth, then return it to the freezer. Repeat the process twice more.

You can't beat handmade chocolate truffles. They are one of heaven's gifts and should be savored as one of the wonders of the modern chocolate world.

chocolate truffles

8 oz. best quality dark chocolate (at least 70 percent cocoa solids), chopped into tiny, even-sized pieces about the size of a coffee bean (1⅓–1½ cups)

¾ cup whipping cream

2¼ cups unsweetened cocoa powder or confectioners' sugar, for rolling

a 14-inch pastry bag fitted with a ½-inch nozzle

a baking tray or cutting board covered with plastic wrap

MAKES ABOUT 50

Put the chocolate in a large heatproof bowl. Put the cream in a saucepan and bring to a bubbling boil. Remove from the heat and let it subside for 1 to 2 minutes, then pour it over the chocolate. Stir well with a wooden spoon until the chocolate is melted and smooth. To follow Method A, let the mixture cool to room temperature—at least 30 minutes; or, to follow Method B, chill the mixture in the refrigerator for 1 hour.

Method A When cool, beat the mixture with a hand-held electric mixer or a balloon whisk until the mixture just begins to hold. The beaters should barely leave a trail when lifted out of the mixture. Don't over-beat or it might separate and become difficult to manage. Don't worry if you think it is still a little soft—it soon firms up. Spoon the mixture into the pastry bag and pipe small truffle balls, about 1½ inches diameter, onto the covered baking tray or board. Refrigerate for about 1 hour.

Method B When the mixture has set in the refrigerator, remove the bowl and let the contents come to just below room temperature. Using a teaspoon or a melon baller, scoop out bite-sized spoonfuls and transfer them to the covered baking tray or board.

Whichever method you use to make the truffles, continue as follows. Coat the palms of your hands with confectioners' sugar, then roll the truffles into balls. Alternatively, roll them in cocoa powder. Store in an airtight container in the refrigerator until ready to serve.

Variations
* Instead of coating the truffles in cocoa powder, you can dip them into tempered couverture (see page 22). Use a proper dipping fork if you have one, otherwise a normal fork will do the trick. Drop the chilled truffles into the bowl of tempered chocolate, then lift them out with the fork. Tap the bottom of the truffle on the side of the bowl as you draw it out and put it on the covered baking tray or board.

* You can also add ¼ to ⅓ cup alcohol of your choice after the chocolate and cream have been thoroughly mixed.

This modern version of the centuries-old drink called *xoco atl* is not only more desirable and attractive than the original, but it is a considerable taste sensation.

drinking chocolate

2 oz. dark chocolate (at least 70 percent cocoa solids), grated or finely chopped

1 cup whole milk

1 tablespoon heavy cream

TO SERVE (OPTIONAL)

the seeds of 1 vanilla bean

½ teaspoon finely ground pistachio nuts

MAKES 1 GENEROUS CUP

Put the chocolate in a heatproof bowl. Put the milk and cream in a saucepan and bring to a boil. Remove the pan from the heat and let the milk subside. Pour a small amount of the hot milk and cream over the chocolate and stir to a smooth paste. Gradually pour in the remaining milk, stirring gently all the time, until the chocolate is melted. Let stand for several minutes to infuse completely.

Return the chocolate milk to the pan and reheat gently. Do not let it boil or it may separate. Remove the pan from the heat, whisk to a foam with a balloon whisk, then pour into a cup. Sprinkle the vanilla seeds or the pistachios over the top of the foam, if using, and enjoy.

Use the best quality cocoa powder you can find. The heat of the chili takes this chocolate drink to another dimension!

hot chocolate

2 teaspoons best quality unsweetened cocoa powder

2½ cups whole milk, or 1¼ cups milk mixed with 1¼ cups light cream

1 teaspoon chopped dried chili or ½ teaspoon chopped fresh chile

a pinch of sugar (optional)

SERVES 2

Put the cocoa powder in a heatproof bowl, add about 1 tablespoon of the milk, and mix to a smooth paste with a wooden spoon.

Put the remaining milk, or milk and cream, in a saucepan, add the chili, and bring to a boil. Carefully strain the boiling milk onto the cocoa paste through a fine-mesh strainer, then whisk vigorously. Pour into 2 generous china cups (I think it always tastes better served in porcelain). Let it cool for about 1 minute, then taste—you may need to add a pinch of sugar. Serve immediately.

WHERE TO BUY GREAT CHOCOLATE

Amedei
29 Via San Gervasio
56020 (La Rotta) Pisa, Italy
+39 (0)587 484849
www.amedei.it
*Heavenly chocolate from Tuscan
brother and sister team, Alessio and
Cecilia Tessieri. Stocked by:*
Marie Belle, 484 Broom Street
New York, NY 10013
212-925-6999
Market Salamander
200 West Washington Street
Middleburg, VA 20117
540-687-8011
The Epicure Market
1656 Alton Road
Miami Beach, FL 33139
305-672-1861
Fog City News
455 Market Street
San Francisco, CA 94105
415-543-7400
Surfas Inc., 8824 National Blvd.
Culver City, CA 90232
310-559-4770

Bissinger's
4742 McPherson Avenue
St. Louis, MO 63108
314-367-9750, 888-247-7464 (toll
free), 800-325-8881 (toll free)
www.bissingers.com
*Quality hand-crafted truffles, boxed
chocolate, and seasonal specialties
using top quality ingredients, from
the country's oldest chocolatier.*

Black Hound
170 Second Avenue
New York, NY 10003
212-979-9505
www.blackhoundny.com
*A highly regarded artisanal
chocolatier with a unique line
of truffles and confections.*

L.A. Burdick Handmade Chocolates
P.O. Box 593, Main Street
Walpole, NH 03608
800-229-2419 (toll free)
www.burdickchocolate.com
*This high-end artisanal chocolatier
uses top quality chocolate and local
ingredients to create unique truffles,
candies, and confections.*

Chocolat Céleste
2506 West University Avenue
St. Paul, MN 55114
651-644-3823
www.chocolateceleste.com
*Using fresh, local ingredients, and no
preservatives, Chocolat Céleste crafts
fresh truffles in epicurean flavors.*

Chocolat Moderne
27 West 20th Street, Suite 904
New York, NY 10011
212-229-4797
www.chocolatmoderne.com
*A high-end artisanal chocolatier
creating unique confections and
truffles using old-world techniques.*

Chocolate Springs
The Lenox Shops, Route 7
P.O. Box 1944
Lenox, MA 01240
413-637-0820
www.chocolatesprings.com
*This high-end artisanal chocolatier
creates unique bonbons using
ingredients such as teas, herbs, and
classic flavors.*

Chocosphere.com (Internet only)
5200 S.E. Harney Drive
Portland, OR 97206
877-992-4626 (toll free)
www.chocosphere.com
*A large selection of quality chocolate
and cocoa from around the world.*

Christopher Elbow Chocolate
118 Southwest Boulevard
Kansas City, MO 64108
816-842-1300
www.christopherelbowchocolates.com
*Uniquely flavored and designed
handmade chocolates and truffles.*

Christopher Norman Chocolates
60 New Street
New York, NY 10004
212-402-1243
www.christoperhnormanchocolates.com
*Handmade truffles and bars in a
variety of flavors and textures and
hand-painted special collections.*

Chuao Chocolatier
937 S. Coast Highway 101
Encinitas, CA 92024
760-635-1444
www.chuaochocolatier.com
*Unique truffles and bonbons using
exclusively El Rey Venezuelan
chocolate and quality ingredients.*

Richard Donnelly Chocolates
1509 Mission Street
Santa Cruz, CA 95060
888-685-1871 (toll free)
www.donnellychocolates.com
*Handmade chocolates from European
chocolate and local ingredients.*

Fran's Chocolates
2626 NE University Village St.
Seattle, WA 98105
800-422-3726 (toll free)
www.franschocolates.com
*Unique truffles and bonbons using
a blend of top quality chocolate.*

Garrison Confections
815 Hope Street
Providence, RI 02906
401-490-2740

www.garrisonconfections.com
*One of the top confectioners in
America offering handmade bonbons.*

**The King Arthur Flour Baker's
Catalog**
Route 5 South, Norwich, VT
800-827-6836 (toll free)
www.kingarthurflour.com
*A catalog and website that sells
excellent chocolate bars and cocoa.*

Lillie Belle Farms
1345 Daisy Creek Road
Jacksonville, OR 97530
541-899-9037
www.lillebellefarms.com
*Award-winning handmade chocolates
using time-honored European methods.*

Payard Patisserie
1031 Lexington Avenue
New York, NY 10021
212-717-5252
www.payard.com
*Excellent quality truffles and
chocolates by an acknowledged
master of the craft.*

Scharffen Berger Chocolate Maker
914 Heinz Avenue
Berkeley, CA 94710
510-981-4066
www.scharffenberger.com
*This is the first company to make
artisan chocolate from the bean in
the US in over 50 years. Quality dark
and milk chocolate.*

Jacques Torres Chocolates
66 Water Street
Brooklyn, NY 11201
718-875-9772
www.mrchocolate.com
*Produces artisan confections and
bonbons and house-made chocolate.*

INDEX

conversion charts

Weights and measures have been rounded up or down slightly to make measuring easier.

Volume equivalents:

American	Metric	Imperial
1 teaspoon	5 ml	
1 tablespoon	15 ml	
¼ cup	60 ml	2 fl.oz.
⅓ cup	75 ml	2½ fl.oz.
½ cup	125 ml	4 fl.oz.
⅔ cup	150 ml	5 fl.oz. (¼ pint)
¾ cup	175 ml	6 fl.oz.
1 cup	250 ml	8 fl.oz.

Weight equivalents:

Imperial	Metric
1 oz.	25 g
2 oz.	50 g
3 oz.	75 g
4 oz.	125 g
5 oz.	150 g
6 oz.	175 g
7 oz.	200 g
8 oz. (½ lb.)	250 g
9 oz.	275 g
10 oz.	300 g
11 oz.	325 g
12 oz.	375 g
13 oz.	400 g
14 oz.	425 g
15 oz.	475 g
16 oz. (1 lb.)	500 g
2 lb.	1 kg

Measurements:

Inches	Cm
¼ inch	5 mm
½ inch	1 cm
¾ inch	1.5 cm
1 inch	2.5 cm
2 inches	5 cm
3 inches	7 cm
4 inches	10 cm
5 inches	12 cm
6 inches	15 cm
7 inches	18 cm
8 inches	20 cm
9 inches	23 cm
10 inches	25 cm
11 inches	28 cm
12 inches	30 cm

Oven temperatures:

110°C	(225°F)	Gas ¼
120°C	(250°F)	Gas ½
140°C	(275°F)	Gas 1
150°C	(300°F)	Gas 2
160°C	(325°F)	Gas 3
180°C	(350°F)	Gas 4
190°C	(375°F)	Gas 5
200°C	(400°F)	Gas 6
220°C	(425°F)	Gas 7
230°C	(450°F)	Gas 8
240°C	(475°F)	Gas 9

acknowledgments

I would like to thank everyone who shares my passion for chocolate, especially my husband Richard and my dog Cocoa —although sadly he can only dream about it! Thank you to Michel Roux OBE at the Waterside Inn for showing me the secret of "real" chocolate all those years ago; to Claire Clark MCA (Master of Culinary Arts) "super chocolate and pastry supremo" at The Wolseley; to Alessio and Cecilia Tessieri at Amedei in Tuscany for their inspiration and integrity, and for making some of the world's best chocolate; to Alan Porter at The Chocolate Society; and to Susie Billington, friend and colleague at the Academy of Culinary Arts. Finally, to my mother, whose literary talents are in a league of their own.

Thank you also to Alison Starling, Sharon Cochrane, and everyone at Ryland Peters & Small for being so absolutely charming and patient throughout the commissioning and writing of this book and for putting up with my chocolate eccentricities!

The publisher would like to thank L'Artisan du Chocolat and The Chocolate Society.

PICTURE CREDITS

All photography by Richard Jung unless otherwise stated. Pages 11 and 20–21 © Richard Jung; 12 © HIP/Museum of London/TopFoto; 14–15 © Cadbury Trebor Bassett; 17 © Amedei

BUSINESS CREDITS

L'Artisan Du Chocolat: 89 Lower Sloane Street, London SW1 8DA; +44 (0)20 7824 8365; www.artisanduchocolat.com
La Maison Du Chocolat: 45–46 Piccadilly, London W1J 0DS; +44 (0)20 7287 8500; www.lamaisonduchocolat.com
Rococo Chocolates: 321 King's Road, London SW3 5EP; +44 (0)20 7352 5857; www.rococochocolates.com
The Chocolate Society: 36 Elizabeth Street, London SW1W 9NZ; +44 (0)20 7259 9222; www.chocolate.co.uk